ISBN: 979-8-218-49406-3

Helena Rose Publishing
sherosepoetrycollective.com

*From the Author*

# DEDICATION

To my women, my community, my clients, my sister, my mom, the women before and after me.
I love you, I love you, I love you.
This is for us.

Dad- I did it, I love you.
Mom- To the women we are and are becoming.

Maleah, Hailey, Cassie, Alyssa, Kitrina, Kayla, Sarah, Michaella, Mariah, Julie, all my women who healed me, loved me, saw my light even when I felt darkness.
Tanya- for being my safe space to land.
Louis and Rufus- my fur babies for the unconditional love.
Chelsie Diane- the best teacher, my inspiration.

xoxo

# INTRODUCTION

to rise again, and again, and again.

for me this book is a door that has bursted open,
sharing my truth, emerging a woman into her power,
remembering who she is and was.

honoring every emotion and piece of her story.
a door, a key, a lock.

for you, this book can be anything.

it can be a map back to home
a mirror to show you that you are love
a kiss to sleep
a sister telling you to wake the hell up
something to haunt you
or allow you to just say..
me too.

my hope is that you dare to be brave in the world, be
the color when there is black and white, dare to
share your own art.

to live a life worth writing about.
and fall deeply in love with yourself.

# LAST NOTE:

In the last ten years of my life I have grown up in
Idaho moved to a new state, dropped out of college
with nothing,
started three different start ups,
sold a business,
flew across the country to speak,
adopted my fur babies,
worked 50+ hour work weeks, lost loved ones
fell back in love with poetry
ended relationships
struggled with mental health
and the amount of love I have for this world
how to express it and alchemize it.

so here we are on this journey together:

a series of poems and stories, moments I have been
writing since I was 16 years old.

I hope you know this journey is messy, difficult,
beautifully raw, a lesson, not an ending.

permission to question everything.
permission to live your life brilliantly, an ongoing
adventure.

and that you are not, and have never been alone.

P H A S E

# ONE

BURN

# September 27th

Five years ago

on September 27th I said yes

to a dream of a past life of mine

I couldn't eat that night because I believed

I had butterflies

it was the night I thought was a promise

for the rest of my life


now for the first time its about me

my finger feels more free

but so does my soul

for finally choosing me


September 27th is the day I promised to say yes

to every piece of me

and today I chose my heart

and my poetry.

# My truth

This is my truth

I am done with my shit

and claiming my big emotions are too much to handle

that my empathy is my weakness

this is the truth about me claiming my power

that I can feel so deeply

and understand the human race

understand grieving past lovers

I have already died a thousand times

to be here cycling through the seasons

to be fall, to be summer, to honor winter

that my depth is my power

it is not my weakness

and it is not my grave

my sadness is my depth to filled with abundance

and a life lived

where I feel everything

I can connect with souls silently

honoring women with where they have been

and where they are going

my job here is not done

I am Her

who creates life

gives life

has felt the sorrow

who has also brought color

to a world that is black and white


I will no longer accept mediocre as a payment


I am no victim

my sex

my heart

my soul is enough

to fly off the ground again and again

to remind you that you can fly too

this story is not done

and it will not be boring

but brilliantly lived alive.


you are already the poetry.

# Messy little thing

It's okay to be a storm

you can't tame a hurricane

shake the goddamn house down

rattle the windows

scream, let it all out

give yourself grace

let yourself be messy

have big energy

because you've outgrown

your small town city

I hope they gossip about you until sundown

maybe they will learn

that it's healthy

to be a hurricane

rattle their lives

and escape..

# Ready

I broke her open
and I poured out
a tidal wave came roaring in
but the world wasn't ready
for everything
you're about to give.

# Surviving

Of course you were tired
you were surviving for far too long..

have you remembered the journey
you took to get here?
its time to take a pit stop
and pause.

# Lingering

Love is like melted chocolate dripping down your throat

orgasmic

salty, bitter, sweet

the taste lingers

the desire for more overcomes you

its a treat

its an addiction

you say just one more..

# Light us up

I lit the match

we both knew you couldn't carry the responsibility

but someone had to

you played the victim

I played the monster

I lit us up on fire

and burned it all to the ground

today is the day I pinky swore

to myself to remember

I no longer have to run into the house on fire

to try to save you

smoke fills my head

I hope I learn to believe in love again

little did I know that this was one chapter

not the end of my book

every season must come to an end because


the show must go on..

# The night

Dark thick fingers curl around my throat

no one thought you would

your eyes black

your heart filled with smoke

they said you were just drunk

too drunk to remember

women too said they witnessed you

who knew you would challenge my power

so afraid of a woman

a man who has to use his hands, is powerless and pathetic

the power lies within me to share your story

I'm not the first women and I won't be the last

what a good friend you were

wrapping your hand around my neck

what a good friend you were

I'm so glad it didn't last.

# Your monster

She dimmed her light for his darkness

a woman who dimmed herself for many men

I don't blame her

like she blamed me

she swore you morphed into the man she craved

that my marked skin was just a mistake

it's been five years since we talked

you blocked me

thank god

men were never your monsters

you made me your monster instead

so the guilt feels lighter when you close your eyes at night

Oh ex best friend,

I'm so glad you blocked me

I'm starting to finally feel happiness again.

# Built differently

From the words vomiting from your gaping hole

of a mouth

after I ripped you up

I thought I found more

but all I found was a vast dark hole

instead of a soul

we were built differently you see

your ego feeds you

and love feeds me.

# Musk

Only you could melt me like butter

a home that felt comfortable

the smell of musk mixed with tequila

is it an addiction or an obsession

that I keep running back to you

for more?

I don't need too

but running into a burning house

is what I am use too

I no longer find comfort in the chaos

and I can't save you.

# Another day

We are all decaying

the wrinkles tell stories on our skin

the needles will only delay

we are all decaying

instead of celebrating

that we got to live another day.

# Deeper

To our love-
deeper than the ocean higher than the sky
we were both wrong about one thing
it was not limitless,
this life

the ocean is only so deep
until you feel like you are drowning inside.

# Impatient

You called me impatient

I waited ten years

for you to finally make a decision

at the finish line you still couldn't decide

there was always an excuse when you couldn't

even show up on time

or when you went to lunch with her

instead of me

it wasn't a date, silly!

what is silly was waiting around

for a boat that never ported

a plane that could never fly

or to listen to your dumbass lies

the clock was still ticking

as I sat in the waiting room

to finally be called

to be the chosen one

after years of waiting

for you to grow up

instead it just got old

your words never matched up with your actions

was I impatient
or did I finally realize
I was done wasting
this one precious life
on someone who
was just wasting my time.

# To the grave

I allowed myself to die

because she wasn't me

she was a mold of what everyone wanted me to be

I built her for years

a model of your dreams

until I put her to sleep

when I woke up

I rebuilt me

the woman whose brave

and speaks her mind

a woman who doesn't need saving

demands respect, and to feel alive

she's a little lion inside

roaring with pleasure, abundance and

taking her time

to rebuild properly

pumping love inside of each cell

expanding every second

thats the story I'll tell

not the past version of me

that you still crave me to be.

# Oh caption..

Oh caption, my caption

I imagine a world with braless women

I imagine a world where tampons are free

I imagine a world where there wasn't war just

beauty..

Don't take advice from people
who haven't left the ground
who are boring
who haven't loved with their whole hearts
or haven't felt heaven and hell
in one life.

# Normal

I was blinded by normal

normal was a lie

it was normal to feel like you wanted to die

to take away your life

at eleven years old

she was young and didn't know

that life had just begun


oh the hug I would give her.

# Your weapon

I will never forget the women who have been killed

by using their voice and speaking their truth

so speak

so scream

so write

word by word

tear down the thousands of years of repression

inequality

roar

because

no wonder you're so afraid

to use the power of your voice.

# Overgrown

I didn't know what was worse at the time
the weeds that multiplied like cancer in my yard
or in my head?

# Stolen youth

You craved the ocean

but you got a drought instead

he says that you're the "one" but only wants you in bed

so you feed his ego and do what you are told..

you thought you were being so brave and so bold

for putting yourself out there,

giving them your body

your soul

trading it for love- so you've been told

they call you a whore, slut, bitch, a hoe

they even high-fived when they knew that they were

eskimo bros

they took and took until they could no more

but now you're twenty six years old

who realized that love wasn't a drought

and you were never a whore

that you create life itself

you are the sun, moon, ocean and sand

you were never the problem

it was the man.

# Distance 25

I need you to be an ocean away to find myself again..

# I forgot to tell you

I forgive you for what you had to do to survive

I forgive you for wanting to die

I forgive you for pretending you weren't a poet

I forgive you for losing yourself in him

I forgive you for pretending

I forgive you for performing

I forgive you for not loving your body

I forgive you for settling

I forgive you for not writing

I forgive you for closing your throat and

not sharing your truth

I forgive you for thinking it was your fault

I forgive you for the times you held your screams in

I forgive you for being afraid

I forgive you for surrendering

I forgive you for pretending everything was ok

I forgive you for dismissing your desires

I forgive you for your depression

I forgive you for not living everyday

I forgive you for the pain that was never yours to carry

I forgive you for not loving yourself.

# Bare hands

I helped her create an empire
with her two bare hands
and you still told her she wasn't good enough
we are not the same.

# Easier

You do a great job at grieving

the tears that stream on your bathroom floor

the pain in your chest feels like it will rip out your soul

hurling every emotion out of your body

questioning your existence

but every time you look in the mirror

you promise yourself

it can only get easier.

# Tired

I am tired of waiting

for commitments

for decisions to be made

I am tired of waiting for the people in my life

to wake up

to love

to live

to cry

to be more than just survive


I am no longer waiting

for you to wake up in this short life.

# Skip

If I had a remote
I would fast forward to the good part
the part where I am not consumed
the hollowness in me is filled
the part where it all makes sense..

# Sewing

The needle pierced the more I sewed
each stitch
was an ounce of self love
sewing my chest back together again.

32

It's time to forgive yourself

of the things

you didn't have to take responsibility for..

# Glow up

They asked how I was doing

with a wandering eye

searching for signs of distress, depression or feeling loss inside

searching for my weakness, my failures

aching to see the pain that has consumed me

but today I didn't even cry

I felt peace for the first time

the sky looks bluer and matches the sea in my dreams

my lungs don't collapse when I breathe

I won't give them the satisfaction of my discomfort


when the truth is

I am more than just fine

I only allow love into my life

only light can touch me

I'm not a damsel in distress

I don't wear a disguise

when it rains

the flowers have to blossom

at some point in time.

# Tending your garden

You poured into others

when you had a drought

you were taught to tend other gardens

before yours

and wondered

why your desires never flourished

while you were stuck with weeds.

# Malibu

My skin licked by the sun

the only thing that kisses me lately

it lingers longer than the kisses you marked my skin with

just a little longer

I crave the curves of my body to be near your mouth

like a tide crashing in

an orgasm on the beach

smiling like a fucking idiot

recollecting our time in Hawaii

Malibu feels different without you

you are a room in my house of life

that I keep wanting to come back to

but I hid the key far away

dropped it in the ocean

my dreams tell me to open the door back up

the canyon spills out and my brain assumes

I'm crawling back

in bed with you

opening the door and spilling my adventures on the table

wishing you could be on this quest with me

I dance on my toes falling over my own feet

learning how to do this dance of life alone
do you ever re-read chapters?
I couldn't tear this one out
I kept it close to my heart as if it were the map
to travel back to you
the only thing that I crave is the sun to kiss my skin
to burn it all away
please burn it all away..

# Checkmate

Hand to my cheek

you smacked me

laughing on the inside

like a joke you've been waiting to tell

I was only eighteen years old

just a little woman who knows how to raise hell

my life advice was created that day

sometimes you need to match their energy

and challenge their play

my hand connected with your cheek

checkmate

wondering how a little girl like me

had the confidence to say

you will never lay a hand on me

or I'll send you to your fucking grave.

# Nobody's soldier

I didn't walk away from the fight

but I will not fight your wars anymore

and sacrificing my life

for dreams that aren't mine

my battle wounds are still healing

cuts run deep, my heart bleeding

scars that will remain

until my last breath

my last day

I'm not your soldier

I can't save your life

when you aren't wiling to even fight.

# Bleeding

To bleed without dying

it's a thirty day occurrence

a cycle that causes me to die

parts of me inside

within my womb

a superpower

a woman can create in this life

I will bleed

without dying

I shed layers

and cleanse every month

to birth, to restart

over again, and again, and again

a self cleaning machine

and you are still afraid of me?

of a little bit of blood?

to be scared of my blood- YOU are scared of my BLOOD

every living cell inside of me

I would be afraid too

because what if its true

God is a woman

would she be stripped away?

unclothed, raw with no rights
over her womb
and every inch of her meat suit
and life?
would my blood still scare you?

# First last day

This is your first last day

of being in survival mode

coping with a cup of poison

burning dollars in pockets

covering your stomach

blaming yourself for the love you gave

this is your first last day

to finally fall back in love with your life.

# Burn it

Blow up your life

piece by piece and when it falls

let it drop where it needs to drop

don't control it

don't try to fix it

let it be messy as all hell

let it crumble

let it all fucking burn

and wait

wait until it turns to ash

to recreate it

and turn it to gold!

# Fired.

Fuck you.

I wanted a better life for us

this is me building it, for me

you are finally fired

you're job was incomplete

the ring burned my finger

it was a promise you could never keep.

You hated my emotions
so I wrote more poetry.
I will never choose to
numb myself
again..

# Poison

Please let me sink my teeth into your skin

and suck out the poison

that causes you this much pain

it's not my mess to clean

depression is a leche

but the light I see in your eyes

reminds me of the time

my life didn't feel like mine.

# Winter in summer

I have frost bite

as the sun burns my skin as it kisses me

to experience winter in summer all in one day

my heart turned to ice the second I left

maybe its been that way

for years now

I didn't know avalanches happened in March

but here we are

in an hell of a winter

the road winds down the path

to the next era

black ice hits us

nothing scares me anymore, anyways

I've wasted away

finally eating for the first time in three days

some would call this the road home

going back to the place I know

I wanted to fight it

to fight you, but there was nothing left

in my heart- a gapping hole of what was

and what could have been

I wanted to scream at you

but I couldn't

you let me just leave, and erase me

let the words burn through my lungs

show you the timeline of every time you took the knife

and cut my heart from the inside out

blaming me for the pain

to lose my voice

to suffocate me

and now you finally want me

the road is too long for you to travel

I'm too far gone

besides

you always preferred winter

and I was a summer all along.

I have scars on my heart from loving you
I only regret not loving myself first.

# Duplicate me

Tinder won't heal you

but you already know that

all it took was 24 hours for you to say "fuck that"

"fuck us", and "fuck me" not replying back

your ego craved connection

and you use to call me impatient

so instead of filling yourself with love

you tried to duplicate it

duplicate me, duplicated us

as if i was a science experiment

a doll you could build

I don't think its love you seek

but the validation of a woman, that left you meek

did you find her?

is she one of the five girls

you sought out to sleep

or I guess what I'm asking is

did you find a luke warm version of me?

# Bucket of beer

A brilliant idea

for a bucket of beer

he thought it could drown

away his tears

one bucket, two buckets..

his friends cheered him on

like he already won

but at the end of the night

he still stalked my page

wondering if I would be there

but sadly my heart costs more

then a bucket of beer.

# A poet

This poem must be written

in a country that allows free speech you would think

more people would listen

but nothing is ever free besides the experiences you write

the poem is meant to be lived

to resurrect the dead

the truth that is too scary to be told

instead of shouting and being loud

we take our pens to the paper

and list our every word

to invent

to create

to share

our truth and a new life for you

this is why a poet is a poet.

for you to pick up your pen

and must write your truth again


because you are a poet too.

# Soul Sister

I asked when you die
if you would mix your ashes with mine
instead we will have a field of trees
where our roots will weave
like how you braided my hair
many times before
each strand kissing it with love
we aren't from the same blood
tho you are my sister,
a part of my soul
healing my heart
you didn't break

you would spend your whole life
if you had to
when he didn't even try.

# Pried myself open

I crawled back inside of me

searching for the parts of me

I hide like a treasure box

filled with memories

that no longer destroyed me

I pried myself open again

piece by piece

and rebuilt my heart

I filled it with the love

I once gave to you.

# Twenty seven

My screams echoed

engolfed by the canyon

bouncing off her walls

desiring to be halted by a sign

or possibly someone

but they didn't travel far

nor long

only a few miles

it took some time

for me to come to the conclusion

that no one could hear me

only me and the ringing in my ears

pulling at me

trying their hardest to consume me

like a blackhole

no one has the key inside my life but me

and I realized at the ripe age of twenty seven

the canyon of my soul

the only one who could hear

was the one screaming herself

I'm a woman of options

as if I had lost this one a long time ago

praying that someone else

could find my anchor

call the medics

do the work for me

I had ignored it for far too long

so on this day

I looked down in my hands

grasping a rusty old key

this whole time.

# To be alive

Am I healing or just learning to live?

waking up to my truth every day

learning to take risks

like losing you

and loving me

understanding the word unconditionally

writing poetry through the pain

learning what I have all gained

it took months of pity parties

to see the gold within the soil

of my life

the diamonds that I am collecting

every time I build an ounce of trust

within myself

am I healing

or am I just finally living?

# This is how you heal

The secret recipe to healing..


your sister blessing your goodbye in the rain

your best friend who loves her farm

listens to you cry catching every tear

London who gave you all the butterflies and believe in life

San Diego who held your love, honored you fully

Amsterdam mess made you feel alive again

your high school best friend who's now your sister

will adopt you into the family and

shower you with unconditional love

your other two best friends

will fly to come and save you picking up your heart

piece by piece

women will fill your mailbox with love letters

and will send you love from around the world

your mom will cheer you on from Michigan

your dad will teach you patience and to run towards joy

your aunt will share your poems with the world

and tell everyone how much love you have to give

your uncle will give you all the pep talks you need

you'll start a business or two

you'll pick up one too many hobbies

travel across the ocean

and write a few hundred poems

publish your first book

but most of all

your people will heal you again and again and again

this is how you heal a broken heart

trust that it will all work out.

P H A S E

# TWO

ALCHEMY

# Saving my life

I think this is me saving my life

airports are my new home

flying finding pieces of me across the globe

my therapy bill tripled

I lost twenty pounds

sold everything I once valued

the drops that are left

are the size of the ocean

expanding by the second

I broke the dam and thought I had nothing left

the mirror doesn't break

when I lay my eyes on me

the floor isn't the lowest part of my day anymore

everything I thought I lost

I found

within myself

I was always my own cure

but I was giving it to you,


I am the medicine

to saving my own life.

# Alchemy

The darkness tried to drown me
but I devoured it
I danced in it
I bathed in it
I found the light in it.

# Trusting again

The world craves to love you
not hurt you
let it in.


it is safe to be loved.

# Not much

I am not much lately

rosey cheeks

sunkissed skin

I have been worn down to the bone

aching to rest within my home

I am building inch by inch

inside of my soul

what's a woman without rest?

your body isn't meant to serve

but to enjoy the time spent on this earth.

# Same train

I rode the same train and expected a different view

years passed and I settled

until I leap off

wiped the dust off

and found a life

that gave me the adventure I craved

finally a new destination

all you have to be is brave

and

jump

off

the

train.

# Fathers daughter

I am not a daddy's girl

I am my fathers daughter

I have his hands

a heart ready to pour

hardwork runs in my blood

I grew up too fast

hyper independent

fueled with persistence

a jack and coke

a challenge.

# Made of

You forgot what you are made of

it's not sugar or spice

i's not naughty or nice

it's loving again when your heart is ice

it's moving hundred miles away to never

be treated like that again

it's looking in the mirror and not hating

the parts of your body that society obsessed over

it's the growing a business out of survival mode

it's the spending thousands on therapy

so you love yourself for the first time.

# Waking up a dead poet

The poetry always comes

but I thought it didn't choose me

that my life was dead

just feeling, reacting, performing the play

every single day

the pen refused to write

I denied and lost sight

thoughts drifted away

a poet has to be someone who has lived

and died many lives

I have lived a thousand in this short time

I was asleep to my own becoming

the woman who writes her truth

and sets herself free

did I choose it, or did it choose me?

I'm finally awake

a poet,

who forgot that her life was meat to be lived

again, and again, and again

and has finally picked up her pen.

What was she like when you finally
fell back in love with her?

# Purpose

She picked up the paint brush

and painted her life with purpose

I am not a hostage to what happened

I fixed myself as if i was a project

waiting to be solved

until my human was showing

I tried to cover up the evidence

as if there is was no light to show your true colors.

# Terrible chaos

Did you hear

she is the one

who walked through terrible chaos

and brought life out of the law of love


the one who takes the mess of a life

and turnes it into a masterpiece


she is a woman

designed to create

to become

and live more freely.

# The perfect date

Let's read Anne Sexton

and drink tequila until sunrise

kiss each other by the fire

while I tell you why I hide my scars

the battle wounds of a hurricane

that hit my life, like the roaring fire

your wounds are hidden too

still healing from a tsunami that detroyed you

fearing and loving

battling the balance

we'll share the lives we have lived

then it will happen

your eyes will see the magic in mine

of a woman who gives more

then she has ever received

you'll deny that you'll feel your heart skip a beat

was it the tequila

or was it me?

that night

you'll have to make the decision

to believe in love again

or run away from the rush of the ocean

that once consumed you
you don't think you can swim, like you use to
the current could drown you
like it has in the past
do you believe you could handle
the flood of my love
when I offer a life vest?

# Forgetting

This morning the wind whispered gently
asking the question you have been waiting for...

"When do you forget to live?"

# The flowers

I didn't kill the flowers

nor the plants I bought last year

I believe this is healing

when my home matches my heart inside.

# Refuse

I refuse

to be a steady stream

predictable is not in my vocabulary

consistent, dedicated indeed

but I am the ocean

a tidal wave

an explorer who got lost and found her way

you'll never guess

what I'll do next

the lines are meant to be contained

to feel trapped

you can't contain me

I'm the wild beast

a bird flying free

rules are meant to be questioned

a life is meant to be lived

to dare to think the universe

is perfect and not created to be messy

I'm a wolf on her hunt

to create.

# Spicy vanilla

You're too spicy to get vanilla

a promise I can keep

choosing from all the options

just like ice cream

I refuse to not suck the marrow

out of this one life

and live it fully alive

its a choice you make each day

like picking out your favorite flavor

what will it be this time

vanilla?

or something more spicy?

# Feel again

If I could capture the feeling and put it in a jar
for safekeeping
to relive the moment again, again, again and again
to feel alive again..

You were never broken

just a cracked vase holding on to too much.

# Permission

He pushed me towards my dreams
and every time I had my doubts
blood in my hair
knuckles covered with dust
it didn't matter if I won the race
he loved me just the same

so I raced harder
and did everything I craved
every fight I lost
every track I ran
even at thirteen years old
I didn't care about the metals or the trophies
I just wanted my dad to be proud of me

calling him in a whole foods parking lot
about to uproot my life again
he says to me with all the love
well you haven't tried it yet
little did I know
the question I would be asking
at twenty seven years old

on this new race of life

his permission and blessing

that even when the fear consumed me

I will still make him proud by just being me

changing my mind

and taking on this new challenge of life

dad,

I think its time

to give myself permission

to be fully happy

and love every cell in my body

I love you.

I love you.

I love you.

# Months pass

I no longer drink about you
but my water bill has tripled
I fill my bath up three times a day
trying to wash you away
my skin is dry and cracked
by the hell you put me through.

# The game

Are you breaking down or breaking open?

it's a similar feeling

when your world feels like its expanding and collapsing

and for a moment

you'll have to make a decision

is this me?

cracking open to receive, the life I desire

or will I allow the pressure to take over

oh how I love a challenge!

besides, after all these years

I've built muscle to uphold

the weight of the world

when she's transforming

I use the pressure to create a diamond inside

refine me

shape me

to be a better human

because this is all a game

you can play it

or get played.

# New friend

My name slides off your tongue flawlessly

you've been practicing it in mirror lately

doing extensive research, preparing yourself

for what a beautiful mess

you might wrap yourself in

what my name represents

memorized the way I move

how multipassionate I am

how I have lived

if there was a test you would get extra credit

you didn't mess up one vowel

sucked on each one like it was the last sip on a hot

summer day

coating your throat

say my name, say my name

again and again

my ears tickle every time you do

say it like its your favorite place to visit

your favorite treat

rate me five stars

with those lips

say my name

in between every kiss
you might understand me
more than I understand you.

# Imagine

Imagine the woman becoming..
becoming her
you begged to be her
you begged to create her.

# Little hippy

The juice of this world makes me so full

quenching for years now

taking in every ounce of her nature

honoring the grass below

you don't have to spend hundreds of dollars on crystals to

heal something

hug a tree

like a little hippy

stop waiting for life to happen

she's happening right now

we are all going to die someday

that's the one promise we have

in the meantime

take care of her

fill her up full with love

be delulu, a little bit crazy

call everything your favorite

smell the damp soil

plant your feet on the ground

mother earth is pulsing

begging you to come around

and learn to breathe again.

# Switch

It was safer in the world to turn every feeling off

but now I found the switch

I choose to be dangerous and love fiercely

to turn on everything

and to be raw

and soulful in a world

where numb is

normal.

# Her nature

Her roots are pushing against the pot

she has contained herself in

she is overgrowing again

losing her footing

breaking glass ceilings

it's in her nature

to always be expanding.

# Measuring

The sun doesn't question if she is bright enough

the ocean doesn't lose sight of its purpose

the flower doesn't worry if its pretty enough

the mountains don't feel ashamed

by the space they take up

your dog doesn't question its love for you


so, why do you..

question your value you have in this world?

# Drivers seat

Your ship has no faith

you claim you are lost at sea

your engine failed

your directions are lost

you claim you are drowning

you claim you want to be saved

just surrender, already

stop looking for an escape

turn on all the emotions

and tackle them head on

your fear has been in the drivers seat

for far too long.

# Great grandma

The world stopped
looking outside my front door
I look for little miracles
and find magic in the darkest places
I found you
a little red robin
reminding me of simplicity
of life
every breath
every feather you grew
is a reminder of you
that you are still with me
even on my darkest days..

I love you.

# Be love

If you call yourself love than be love

if you call yourself a writer than write

if you call yourself abundant than take up space

so name yourself for what is true

you're not the depression

the sadness

the unworthy soul you thought you were

you are human

you are light

you are love


this is the truth.

# Open

Open your eyes

my god

lift your gaze from the ground

stop being so afraid of your power

it can stop time

make someone fall deeply into the hole of your soul

a magical spell you put on this world

your gaze, your power

the key to connection

look in the mirror and see the power

of a woman's eyes

they tell the stories of her lifetime.

# The gift

The life she gave herself

was the best gift she could receive

and no one else could give her that.

She is Christmas.

She is champagne.

She is every celebration made.

# ARE YOU ALIVE

My darling did you know you are alive today?
what a wonderful beautiful thing to experience
today is the day you are alive
I want to take you to the highest peak
and shout until your lungs ache

I'm alive
I'm alive
I'm ALIVE

isn't it magical to be alive,
after trying to survive?

You said logic and reason are what turns you on
I must be a buzzkill.

# For the first time

The way I was living no longer made sense
the scale no longer measured my worth
the earth felt as if it were breathing again
my two grey hairs grew in with pride


the mirror said I love you for the first time..

# I got lost

I blame myself for taking the wrong turn

I got lost

and left parts of me on the trail to burn

thinking I couldn't carry it all

I got lost thinking I had to be small

I got lost for you

I got lost for a love that I could never find

I got lost in order to chose myself

I got lost and it was entirely divine

oh the love I have found

she is love

and she is me

I'm so glad I got lost

to finally find me!

# Sold

We are sold permanence
when this world was built on temporary
this is the price to pay to live.

# Floating rock

Stop trying to mold it

into something it's not

they are human

not an experiment

no matter how hard you love

you can't change their DNA

so find another soul out of the eight billion in the world

that will give you the energy

don't marry a project

or someone else's husband

when you can marry a soul you can grow old with

if you look at the reflect

you might see her in the mirror

the only person you will die with

everything else is just a bonus

on this floating rock


we call our planet.

# What if?

What if you loved yourself so much

that mistake you made

you didn't emotionally abuse yourself for it

you kissed yourself,

forgave

and just moved on?

# Dancing woman

When you start to lose yourself

dance in the street with a woman whose over seventy

in a town that looks like Schitt's Creek

there's a softness in her eyes

her wrinkles that crease tell you

that she has lived her best life

so why not dance until your feet fall off

it might not cure your depression

but you'll start to realize that age is just an impression

to be as young as you want

and live a life full of joy

because you never know when the end is near

you might as well live without a care.

# Queendom

How do you rule your queendom?

a throne made of beauty and gold?

or, do you respect yourself enough

to rule your own heart

to have boundaries made of stone

to protect women and children

and walk into the fire

how do you protect this life of yours?

do you walk in the clouds?

or in the battle?

fight wars and save your people?

a solider wants a leader

who walks through fire

has it in her eyes

carries the scars and survives

she's not all beauty

but she is divine

she is a queen

a free spirit

who has claimed her throne

built on bravery, integrity

and not just gold.

# Pint Size People

They whispered there was no ocean inside of you
you were a drop of water that turned into a heavy stream
that ran into a lake
that connected to the goddamn ocean
you were just a drop in their eyes
they underestimated your true potential
the ocean roaring inside of you
a lesson was learned that day,

don't let pint size people determine your worth.

# Bar talk

I asked him the last time he cried
stupid American he slurred back at me
as if he lived a life in his late sixties
refusing to admit he is human too
stupid is a man who brags about his ego
making a living off of parking tickets
you have no depth when your only accomplishment
is the disconnection of the human experience-

we are not the same.

# Important

Kiss me

and you will see how important I am

I should be the first line on your to-do list

a temple to be honored

your favorite holiday to celebrate

you'll mark me on your calendar

kiss my feet

bow to me

love me

again and again..

are you still questioning

how important I am?

The seas will part with my presence

you've never met a woman like me

this independent

I'll expand you, be your match

create worlds that impact

can you measure up to be apart of my world?

or will you think

that I am just

another

silly girl.

# Bruises

Will you pin me down and leave love bites

that won't go away?

will you kiss every inch of my soul?

wrapping me tight with a blanket of warmth

will you moan at the sound of your own name

leaking down my throat?

will you unknot me and swallow me whole?

or am I too big you will choke?


don't you dare be like the others

it's hard to find someone that can hold

all this energy of mine

to crack my code

to soak in my smile

to hold my gaze

for longer than just awhile

will you see the magic in my hazel eyes?

and trust that there are hidden worlds inside?

that will take years to understand

will you stay for that long?

or will you leave before the bruises are gone?

# You get to heal this..

It's an honor to be the woman to heal every

ounce of her DNA

to take responsibility for the shit that wants to stay

to release and purge every single bit of the

weight that is holding you to the ground

to release the chains that could never break

your ancestors

your angels would be so fucking proud

you will not live like them

you are more free

the cave you hide in will collapse

and you will never go back

no longer hiding, waiting to be saved

this isn't a damn Disney movie

trying to change the beast into a prince

you change yourself first

instead of working on another human as a project

you get to heal all of it

every ounce of it

it's a war you are fighting

you take it on day after day

promising your daughters a life where

they never have to wear the same chains

that held you down until this very day

you're finally feeling

all the love and the anger

you use as tools to create a new world

this is your own damn life

enjoy it

make love to it

and honor the way healing is a river

flowing to a new beginning

because it's an honor to heal.

# Gallon size human

He had a pint
you had a gallon
spilling from your heart and soul
no wonder he couldn't love you
he couldn't fill you if he tried.

If you didn't want me to write about you
then you shouldn't have fucked me so good
or fucked me over so badly...

Take responsibility.

# Chasing

You spent so much time chasing
what if you just let it find you for once?
isn't that how love works?

# Race

I came alive

with little to no grace

messy as hell

no longer trying to win the race

I will heal loudly

unapologetically this time

like most women

I have suffered in silence for far too long.

# Thorns

Petty isn't my middle name

rose with thorns that blossoms on graves

graves of old lovers

turning the heartbreak to alchemy

the thorns that prickle before you find the beauty

I won't smash your car

I won't stalk your page

but i'll leave you unblocked

to watch your rainy days

not for the bitter emotions but to be selfish indeed

I like to perform alchemy you see


you are my muse

a wild beast untamed

trying so hard to forget my name

you thrash and you twist

you hiss in clear day

you mask the pain as you try to not

devor yourself and keep sane

my muse indeed

as it starts to rain

the sun peaks in as I pick up the pen
and write again
another poetry prompt
the best revenge.

# Thank you

You were the best teacher

it took me years to learn

I was the student trying to please you

and make you proud

it took me awhile to realize

that all the pain you put me through

brought me closer to someone who

I have craved to become

it took you almost breaking me

piece by piece to rebuild

my soul

you were the best teacher

because you gave me the hardest challenge

to love me more

than I loved you

to finally saving my own life

and I want to thank you.

and I forgive you.

the pain was my power

to evolve,

to create a new life

.

thank you for every mistake you made

I could hate you,

and I did for awhile

until I realized you were never meant to stay.

# Fed up

I am fed up over my fear

I have raged and broken my life

tearing and clawing at my mind

trying to escape the nightmares

through the night

a ghost in my own body

I will no longer fuel my fear

the locks are changed

she's not welcomed here

to be understood and heard

was all she begged for

I hand her the mic

and allow her to speak

piercing and holy

I realized I was never angry with you

more so with me

you were my mirror

in what I really desired to see

I denied myself for years

to be selfishly unapologetic

not people please

or be the rug

I feared to make choices
and be the "good girl" of the story
freezing at the sight of a bad reputation
how dare I want to devour my dreams
only if I looked the way society wanted me to be
now we are here
finally devouring my fear
and becoming selfishly me.

PHASE

# THREE

RISE

# Remembering her

Poetry is an amazing lover

a old friend who welcomes you with open arms

she never stays past eight am

her hair is a mess tangled with her dreams

you take her to dinner- she doesn't wear shoes

dances in the pond, orders three desserts

she marries herself over and over again

she pays with heart-shaped rocks,

and handwrites her love letters, kisses each one with gold

she goes to where the life is

she gets lost with no plan

her heart and her brain bicker but her heart always wins

she doesn't mow her grass

never got the memo about marriage, contracts or religion

unpredictably flying to each corner of her soul

the pen is her best friend

she makes you think differently

your brain inches while your heart melts

she never leaves any words shackled

and promises only an adventure

always waking up and reminding you

you must live a life worth writing about.

# Strawberries

The strawberries in my garden taught me
one day that you can be red, ripe
and little bit bumpy
your time isn't ticking,
it's just beginning they whispered
don't stop sprouting...

# Cracks

Art is made

to fill the cracks of your soul

you must have cracks big enough

in order

to create and fill.

# The artist

The artist inside of me crawled out

and reclaimed her life

I couldn't stop her

she filled every hole of my heart with art

she brought back my creativity that was stolen away

from the never ending to do list

she burned away the pieces of logic and reason

she told me hold on tight

you are a woman,

a woman made to create.

# Mary Oliver

You train like a warrior
and love like a poet

you prepare for war
while loving the planet

you fight like a savage
and create like an artist

you dream like a goddess
and live like a bird broken free

you can create, be anything that is in your dreams
this is your one precious life,
what are you going to do with it?
its time.

# I believe

I believe in prenups

orgasms everyday

celebrating every win

dumping boys who use A.I to write you poetry

opening doors for little old ladies

never buying pots and pans for a bridal shower

forgiving the couple judging you on margarita

Monday with your girlfriends

believing everyone is in love with you

and falling in love with them too

traveling the world and kissing everyone with an accent

writing poetry about everyone and everything

speaking your truth

making messes with this little life

taking a 2pm bath and


living again and again...

# Paint her

Paint her aging skin that has held onto the memories

of traveling the world with a carry on

sending love letters with spilled ink

creating her life

over and over again

let the brush do the talking this time

please don't forget to

paint her aura

her magic

her scars

paint not her beauty, but

what her body holds within her curves

a life well lived

most of all

most importantly

paint her


A

woman

who

was

BRAVE.

# Expecting

You have the capacity to feel everything and

become anything

you thought your art was dead

but you have become

a soul quenching for water

its the sickness we end up surviving

when we had an ocean to give

and they only had a drop and

still expected a thank you.

# Replant

The earth doesn't move for you
but your words
your love
can heal the world
and replant the soil.

# Grace

Your awakening

is your grandma

your moms

and many other women, sisters before you

they planted the seeds to allow you to sprout and grow


give them grace.

# Not this time

Nobody is falling in love this summer

not this time

we have shit to do!

this isn't a music video

a sappy romcom

a Disney movie with a happily ever after

I'm the main character

I don't need a love story

or a hero

I'm on a mission with no distractions

but what is life without love?

of course we could

but we wouldn't dare

that would feel too alive

we would have to be afraid to love again

it would be too soon

I'm not "healed" enough for you

you're messy

you're broken

you're a piece of art

a masterpiece where the paints are meshing together

I would pay twenty dollars to wait in line

and stare at you for hours

wondering how could you be

so beautiful

so messy

so defined

the strokes of your curves

the colors in your eyes

a work of art

that's hard to find

you would be my newest collectible

I would be your obsession

share you with the world

this is why I can't fall in love with you

because when I do..

you would have to fall in love with

me too.

# Illiterate

How odd

I wrote so many poems

but you could never read poetry

there is so much inside of me

bursting out on each page

it would take hours to unravel me

some have tried

and almost died

they are just words to you

but magic to me

it's not my fault

you could never read poetry..

I will never be black and white

only color

bleeding out of my veins

onto each piece of paper.

# Late night

He says he's a mess and a shit show

I don't believe him, what a liar!

his scars are wounds of a warrior

but my god I am too

pieces of our hearts scatter on the floor

broken glass everywhere

we spent all night

gluing

receiving

sharing

the tricks to piece them together

as we cracked the code

to healing each others souls.

# YOU

I'm writing about love again

my therapist says it a win

my dreams don't haunt me anymore

they give me clues like a scavenger hunt

to find the way back to you

what it would feel like to feel calmness

I envy your dogs spot in your bed

my god!

my brain takes over, my heart melts

there's fear in my veins, pulsing with every thought

it felt like sunshine

the heat in my blood

a cat purring through every lick

every love bite, every kiss

you matched my energy

you held it without crumbling

you honored every inch of my soul

I questioned it,

how could you fill my glass so full?

I was told I was so much

so fucking heavy to hold

but you were strong enough

to embrace every ounce of me

my flaws were your perfections

I threw every piece of me at you

hoping you wouldn't catch it

I'm such a sap

and can't fall in love this fast

I'll gaslight myself to believe

it was just a thing

but I think you fell a little in love with me too

because why wouldn't you..

136

You felt like poetry
raw
full of soul.

# Gaining

A misty morning

brings a new potential

to clear the day

I spent too long focusing on the perfections of life

complaining about rainy days

I realized that it was never about the rain

or how I hate reading the end of books

or airport goodbyes

I hate leaving because I thought it was the end

instead it's a new beginning

everything serves a purpose

even when you took a knife to my heart

I bleed out for weeks

and washed away the poison you put in me

I pulled it out crying at every twist

I thought I had dug my grave and lost everything

but I would have missed the life I was suppose to live

I fell more in love in four months

than I have in my entire life

the end was the best part to allow me to realize

there's always a new beginning

a rebirth

I didn't have to dig my own grave

to find out

that I didn't have to die from the pain

I rebuilt my DNA

and got out of the weeds


questioning,

what if I gained everything?

# Paths

Hope is wishing our paths crossed again

where the bridge meets

the gates open up

to experience you again in this life

maybe it will be the day

where I can fully love you..

# A past life

Our souls were lovers in a different life

maybe it started at the coffee shop window

I had the courage to walk inside

we then deeply feel in love with each others eyes

wouldn't it be wild

to daydream about our past time

you would know my middle name

and take me out once a week

become lovers

have a baby

and name her Diane after your great aunt

we would have traveled the world

I would write you poetry

you would be the cook of the family

we would fight about stupid little things

like a old couple

my god what a simple beautiful life we lived

maybe we got bored

and I desired more

but in this life we are just strangers

staring into each others souls

on the streets of London

I know it is you because time stopped again
but this time I moved on
this is not the life where I devote it all to you
was it a mistake?
that it couldn't be us?
and it couldn't be you?

# Future lover

I just want to burn a candle let it drip into

the hours of the night

your head laying heavy on my thighs

as I read you every line

from every poem I created

within this life

and secretly have you guess..

become so OBSESSED

and think every single one is about you

because what if it is?

I want you to hang on every word

sipping every last drop of every line

my dream is for you to understand

why I write

my future lover

will buy me a ring

and a blank brown book

to fill every line, every page

about the way you love me everyday

write about how you

filled me up and believed in my soul

you'll say to me
wiith tears in your eyes
I was truly your best investment
in this short little life.

# Moan

Do you also moan

when you step into the sunlight

when she kisses you

your body exposed

where do the lips land

you can practice on me, and see

what makes my mouth yawn

and give me an o

do you moan when I say your name

when you taste me

or are you selective

and shy

and hold back the air in your chest

not even make a little peep

to never let someone hear

the pleasure you release

on this earth

a soft hurricane in your body

begging to be released

all I ask is tonight

will you moan for me?

# Choicing

The path only gets old when you are dizzy going in circles

the blisters start welting, peeling, bruising

you're crawling on your knees

bleeding out piece by piece

your soul

too afraid to take a different way

but no one told you

or maybe you lost hearing

but let me just say

everyday you are just digging your own grave

don't die in your nine to five

selling your soul to some earthly goal

to earn a 401k at what cost?

for your heart to decay..

safety comes from within

and whatever you desire to create

please do me a favor and quit everything you fucking hate

live for the days that you never want to end

explore every corner of the earth

the money will find you, she's codependent and loves you

it will all be worth it

even if it takes stumbling on your feet
to learn how to dance in the fire
to feel your chest expand within every cell
there is no magic ball
just a better path
to choice your dreams.

# Little one

You are now the woman that takes care
of that little girl inside of you
make her proud.

148

In the garden filled with thrones be the wild rose..

# This little life

I have lived a thousands lives in this lifetime
and I have loved every version of her.

# Colorado

When the glass was empty I moved to Colorado

she watered the soil

she taught me how to tend my garden again

she let me stumble and find the light

she didn't fill my cup,

she shattered it and said no more

she burned the past to the ground

and screamed your worth is bigger than this

fire blazed

out of the ashes

I built my art

I built me.

# Post office man

He told me that I could save eighty cents

if I didn't seal my letters in gold

he told me

money is evil,

remember that when you're old

he told me to save every penny,

hide it away in a deep dark hole

until i realized safety didn't come from empty

men spilling their broken codes

I am magic,

a woman

a woman made of gold

who refused to live in scarcity mode.

# Big

Make your magic very big

touch every room

light yourself up like fire

refuse to diminish

even when the world craves you to be smaller.

# The world I love

I already fell in love with the world!

even when it couldn't love me

bipolar, anxiety, ADHD

label after label

trying to sell me that I was wrong for having

emotions the size of the universe

how is it legal to overmedicate someone like me

when all I needed was someone to listen to my screams,

to believe in my voice

and stop making my trauma my fault and responsibility

I'm crazy, emotional, dramatic

if that's what you want to believe

I'm a poet with an ancient soul

my love feels like a thousand angels hugging you

to go to war with me is sending troops of millions

I feel the depths of the ocean

and the heat of the sun

you labeled my big heart a problem

oh god you called me manic

when you couldn't handle my big dreams

I fell in love with the world

even when it couldn't fully understand me.

# Main character

I am too main character energy to play
a supporting role in your play,
I would have fired me too.

# Ninety four

I'm drunk on love and whiskey

it's only 4am

hair a mess feeling heavenly

I giggle and jump on my feet

I can't wait to be ninety four years old

and tell all the old folks at the senior home

all of my adventures

show them pictures of my travels

my loves, young and old

while sipping whiskey in a teacup that I stole

"MORE!" they'll all scream

thank god I said yes to every single decision

that tingled through my body

we will take a time machine

back to the age of twenty seven

and relive each memory

the only regrets that I will have

is not cutting my bangs

sooner

and not asking myself

when did this life become so delicious?

I became the blessing I craved

through all the pain

to make my wrinkled self smile

and realized I never wasted a life

because it was always mine

I fought for it everyday

and swallowed it whole

I dressed up like Barbie

and created every story I told.

# Wildness

Come cover me with your wildness..

make my throat rumbleee with a roar that

shakes the cabinets

a thunderstorm in my chest that beats a million miles

per minute

show me your wild

your heart that's a savage

to trust your instincts

and lick up your desires like honey on my stomach

cover me in your wild

peel me off the floor

honor me on your apartment patio

on a lake boat we stole

in the bed that has a loose bolt

devore me whole

show me your wild with a language

that tastes tender on your tongue

whisper in my ear you're about to come

tug on the sheets

howl at the moon

let me feel every ounce of your wild

let me be consumed.

# I am still learning

I am still learning to fill my cup

I thought I loved tea

floral, full of flavor

I used a tea spoon to pour

and now I use a gallon

I'm still learning to love myself

write love letters to wake up to

2pm bathes to wash the stress away

I thought I was hard to love

until I poured all my love on myself

my god

it's easy to love me!

# Every version of you

An old hit that plays at the dive bar

reminds you of your early days

we loved how she was naive

and fell for everything

how she lived her life so full

unafraid of the mistakes she might make

every version of you

needs love too

my god how beautiful it is to

evolve

and to love

your past you

its so beautiful

that no matter what

she chose to love

again and again

we love her

little you.

# Black Sheep

If I follow in your footsteps will that be me?

will I end up like you but with more attitude?

I'm here to break generational codes

not to keep copying what is old

I'm the black sheep

the one who shakes and breaks the ground

while she runs towards her next path

I will choose health

I will choose wealth

I will choose to create

I will choose to give my heart away to those in need

I will not follow your footsteps

I am free!

to build the future I want to create

and I'm sorry it's not a path you are comfortable walking

but I'm on a mission that's bigger than the sea

to impact the world

so we can all be a little more free.

# Quenching

I desire that my name will be soaked in your mouth

sucking on every last drop of each syllable

flooding your drought

tasting every flavor and piece of me

like your favorite treat

your soul will be so full

arms extended, ready to receive

you'll say open

open your mouth

your lips

your love will slide down my throat thick, and juicy

taking away the burn of the quench

I've been longing for

open

wider

your lips, your lips, your lips

to be kissed

to be loved

to feel whole

my name will be your favorite word

by the end of the night

the ultimate goal.

# My Rising

How could I be late for my own rising?

I was never late

the clock was off, society pressured me

to have kids at the age of eighteen

to be young and not drink

to get married

to play the part of the happy house wife

but still have a purpose that's not too big

to be the supporting role

you thought I was rising on your time?

I rode at dawn straight for my dreams

I rise every day and stay away from the pressures

of a world that expects me

to stay small and afraid

I will never be a supporting role

I was hired for the lead

no wonder you were never happy with me

my rising is on time

I was never late or early

I only overachieved because

I thought that was expected of me.

# My angels

My angels love me

they are getting drunk on whiskey

they're classy and sweet

they guide me to do it

all for the poetry

they bought a popcorn machine

as if they are watching reality tv

multiplying by the minute

one by one sending me all the love

I need ten thousand angels to guide me

to fight for me

to help me expand every ounce of my being

on this path to victory.

# Mountain

You called me mountain

you called me big

you called me

"I don't even know what to do with you!"

you called me love

you called me hot

you didn't even know my name

you made my insides squirm

you made me smile like a fucking idiot

because I don't even know you yet

but you craved me

to know every inch of my soul

you read me like the bible

Jesus would be proud,

so proud

I thought God wasn't real until I saw him in your eyes

goddess is what i'll call you

he sent you from the heavens to heal my hell

five minutes and you consumed me

I thought I was big

but you swallowed me whole

to be brave

to love again, and again, and again..

# Home

I am home!
I created a sanctuary
a place that feels like home
I can take it everywhere with me


for it is always in my soul..
brick by brick
I filled her with warmth
with love
her walls echoing with laughter
a place where
souls come
to create
and enjoy each other
to heal wounds
and celebrate one another.

# Brave

The bravest woman I know
is a woman in her power
a woman who knows her worth
a woman brave enough to live
a woman who creates alchemy
a woman in her full abundance

she is you and she is me.

# Ride

You are worthy to ride directly towards it
ride to the point where you hit the edge
and decide to fly
the dreams that keep you up at night questioning
this one life
choose option number one
instead of settling for number two, three or thirteen
restart again, and again,
and again
a wise woman once told me
to head directly towards joy
it's the only key that opens all the doors
even the ones you refuse to believe
you are unworthy to enter.

# She was WILD

She was wild

like a boar devouring the earth

a giant ambushing her dreams

remembering her soul

stepping into her planet

she created from

old lovers

and old stories

she turned the ash to gold

my god she was wild

she was a wild woman

listed on her gravestone

she lived her life carefree

her spirit flying across the world

touching each corner,

the center of her universe

was her own soul.

# Receiving my love

To be on the receiving side of my love

is feeling a breeze in the middle of June kissing your lips

to be my muse and spend hours listening

to my poetry written about you

its the breath of fresh air

the smell of cider on a warm fall day

it's the Christmas magic every time I lay my eyes on you


to fall in love with me

is one of the easiest things to do.

# She is me

She remembered who she was

through magic, art, poetry, heartbreak

she traveled across oceans

she conquered seas

she is the woman of my dreams

she is me.

# SHE ROSE

like a lion out of her cave

bursting into the brilliance that she is

the darkness couldn't devour her

the sadness choked while trying to swallow her

depth in her soul she is the alchemy

and the poem

she is the art, deciding to rise


Again, and again, and again...

# My love letter to you

You are love,

You are worthy to receive everything you desire

You are worthly to pour your pain out on paper

You are worthy to sweat for your dreams

You are worthy to heal the world with your love, with your gifts and medicine

You are fire, you were never bad for feeling anger

Use the anger to create, to love harder and fight harder

You are inspirational beyond belief

You are self controlled, intelligent, you must trust your brain and heart again

You must allow yourself to be human, and let go of the guilt

You are wild, and free to create

You deserve to feel and create everything

You are here to experience this whole existence

You can get rid of everything you hate

You can choose to only allow love to touch you

You were never bad, you are love

You are worthy of working hard for your dreams

You have permission to change your mind at anytime and pivot again and again..

You are worthy to feel it inside of you again
Your love is meant to be bigger
Your perspective is meant to be changed
You might die today, we don't know when
but you deserve to live it fully alive
You are worthy of living a life of integrity, bravery
You are worthy to speak up, speak your mind, use your voice
You are worthy to be the magic this world needs

Promise me this–
You must do all the things you think you cannot do
You must do it with fear, and set yourself free from the box
society tried to contain you in.

You get to choose,
bravely choose that starting today only love gets to
reach you and that you get to be the color in a world of
black and white.

I hope you live a thousand lives in this lifetime.
and be the wild rose among the thrones.

with all the love
xoxo,
Helena Rose

Hi, I'm Helena Rose
A multiple passionate woman, CEO, writer , dog lover, and traveler.
I help women around the world write their truth, create their lives
and fall in love with themselves again through the power of poetry,
and scaling businesses. The poems in this collection are the result of
my encounters with the complexities of life, mental health, love, and
the human experience of a woman rising and remembering her
power.
Ultimately, her journey remembering who she is and who she can
become. Being the color in a world that is black and white

I hope you find a piece of your own journey in these verses and took
what you needed. Changing the world one poem at a time.

Cover illustrations by Maleah Wininger
*Join my membership..*
**www.sherosepoetrycollective.com**